4 LONG
LARS PALM

Newton-le-Willows

Published in the United Kingdom in 2019
by The Knives Forks And Spoons Press,
51 Pipit Avenue,
Newton-le-Willows,
Merseyside,
WA12 9RG.

ISBN 978-1-912211-40-1

Copyright © Lars Palm, 2019.

The right of Lars Palm to be identified as the author of this work has been asserted by them in accordance with the Copyrights, Designs and Patents Act of 1988. All rights reserved. No part of this publication may be reproduced, stored in a retrieval system, transmitted in any form or by any means, electronic, photocopying, recording or otherwise, without prior permission of the publisher.

Acknowledgements:

a shorter version of (**that standard face**) was first published in *Truck*
(**hastings**) first appeared in *swirl*

contents

(adventures with zombi)   7

(that standard face)   15

(dear letter)   29

(hastings)   45

4 LONG

(adventures with zombi)

chapter i

it's unclear to the zombi who invented it or if it invented itself

chapter ii

it's unclear to the zombi if this means it has an identity crisis & if that is passing or ongoing

chapter iii

what's clear to the zombi is that it's way past caring or at least expected to be

chapter iv

another thing that's clear to the zombi is that it cares little what gender is ascribed to it & that it would love to have that space left blank in its passport

chapter v

one day our zombi meets another zombi on a street corner in their ghost town & they take a liking to eachother the way only zombis do. so to celebrate they go to a restaurant but get miffed when they can't find human brains on the menu

chapter vi

trapped in the far north our zombi is impatiently waiting for something it might recognize as spring as in days warm enough to remove its feet & let the breeze fill its shoes

chapter vii

it seems our zombi is getting confused

chapter viii

it's apparent our zombi isn't bothered by that

chapter ix

somebody decides to give our zombi a camera. that somebody wants to know what a zombi might see through a lens. it is made very clear to our zombi that there are no strings attached to the camera

chapter x

for some reason & a couple of hours apart our zombi gets photos of 2 single children's shoes lost on sidewalks. what's up with that, it wonders. how hard can it be keeping track of a shoe?

chapter xi

our zombi decides to check if its voice is present today with a longish yay. the living look on in despair

chapter xii

in a moment of clarity our zombi steals one of the strings from a guitar thinking so that's what it meant

chapter xiii

our zombi thinks itself completely apolitical. however it didn't care much for either papa or baby doc. it claims that's because it didn't like their brains but we know that's just a justification

chapter xiv

what's that says our zombi looking at a fire extinguisher

chapter xv

a pen, a pen. my undead kingdom for a pen exclaims our zombi upon learning various alternative uses for them

chapter xvi

our zombi walks into a bar, orders a glass of chivas, downs it in one gulp & leaves. 10 minutes later it returns & repeats

chapter xvii

one of these days i may occupy your kitchen & do a huge shupska salad, says our zombi. that is cucumber & tomato in large chunks & grated goat (or feta) cheese, some olive oil & a great deal of squeezed lemon & it goes wonderfully with brain

chapter xviii

our zombi stares disbelievingly at a bicycle

chapter xix

our zombi knows only one beckett. he of no known zombis. so when on a monday afternoon it stumbles across somebody's print-out of tom becketts little book of zombie poems our zombi is first surprised & then delighted & spends the rest of the week bragging about being the subject of a little book

chapter xx

our zombi enters government & swiftly dissolves it after eating a few of the best brains. our zombi is very clear about that being a paradox

chapter xxi

one morning our zombi sees a strange thing in the sky. it looks like a big lamp. nobody else seems to notice it so our zombi writes it off as an optical illusion. & yet that feels disrespectful to the lamp. our zombi decides it's time for breakfast

chapter xxii

our zombi goes to the library looking for a book on creative ways of cooking human brains

chapter xxiii

just because there's money that doesn't mean there are brains says our zombi, grabs a wad of bills & takes off for more fertile ground

chapter xxiv

& with that our zombi steps out of this story with a toothless grin & a curse

(that standard face)

stares in
disbelief

    *

will walk
with
       or with
out us

    *

lights a breeze

    *

sends
         ants
     running for
cover

    *

hoists a rag for
    reasons unknown

    *

stops sending them
equations

    *

stands
taller than the

tower of
your choice

    *

is a mango
    yes really

    *

needs some
help
dealing
    with
that

    *

    has some
strong pills
      in a pocket

    *

sets new
    standards
for statues

    *

went about
its business

with terrible
amounts

of energy

  *

resists re
designing this
skirt
   & that
revolution for
commercial use

  *

buries a
pair of
   shoes in a
public waste
basket

  *

would not have
thought that
construction

work was quite
that unsafe in
this day & age

    *

applies

no rules

to oranges

    *

reads some
    thing in the
paper
about a new
    book
object

    *

would
not think

so

    *

knows this
country

            is an
affliction

            *

is clean
shaven

            *

is seriously
            considering
genocide

            *

sees a connection
            there

            *

waits for the
            promise of rain

            *

rearranged by
government

approved tear
gas canisters

            *

couldn't
resist smiling
at the great

dane in the
        melancholy
portugese capital

    *

standing firmly
          on some
      body else's
foot

    *

thought up
this great
conspiracy

    *

loves jumping
       up & down in
muddy puddles

    *

hit by
>	heavy
>	rains in
istanbul

>	*

claims it
didn't start
>	the fire

>	*

says i did

>	*

says you did
this & that

to people

it can't name
or describe

>	*

acts
surprised
at the
>	sound

a knee makes
chaos
    & the rain
went to bed

    *

rejected

several
grand ideas

    *

doesn't re
member if
it suffers

from short
    term

memory
loss

    *

stands
before a

jury charged
    with identity
theft

    *

brings
the sun

down
& the
rain

up out
of the pond

    *

opens the
curtain
on a brick
       wall

    *

is
not a
citizen

    *

asks if
      you
believe

in sanity

    *

eats an
orange while
watching the

moon
take a running
jump

    *

looks at you

    *

sits down
    on the side
walk waiting
for a bus
    & avoids
getting
arrested

    *

plans on
    be
coming a river
      running
through
    a town of
your choice

    *

takes an after
      noon stroll
to the harbour

    *

harbours some
seriously
      strange
ideas about
what
      makes a
cosmic
experience

    *

turns a
round to
get a
good
look at

that voice

    *

stars
in a
movie
      called
disbelief

(dear letter)

dear alba,

or dawn or sunrise or whatever local name you may have. we don't meet very often but when we do it's never less than interesting

---

dear anarchism,

we could collaborate nicely reinventing the concept of solidarity & destroying capitalism & all structures of power. how about we meet up tomorrow at, say, 11.55 am?

---

dear arabic,

you didn't know i was going to try to get to know you, did you? those notes from the first class are a first class mess but some time i'll be able to at least read you & say i don't understand & will you please speak a bit slower & get food & a roof over my head. beginning at this age i don't expect, but hope, to be able to hold coherent conversations on topics such as poetry, politics & philosophy. first i have to be able to think in you to avoid having to translate everything before speaking. that's a tall order, though you never know

dear art,

you may be minimalist & then you're not garfunkel or you may be baroque & then you're most likely not impressionist or you may be anatomically incorrect horses & guns & cannon fodder & then you really kick some tender behind

---

dear beard,

you're trendy now. that's nice. but you know you can still strike terror into the hearts of men

---

dear book,

don't worry. just like with punk there are many among us who will not allow you to die

---

dear brat,

beware of the baseball bat & that punk swinging the stairs or the stars hanging on the bar with the door barred dear cat,

it's great that you collect those bird carcasses. what do you suggest we do with them?

———————

dear cops,

cease

———————

dear curiosity,

please stay away from that cat. if instead you pair up with rage & maybe confusion you may well end up as knowledge & then you will become the worst nightmare ever of the powers that be. & maybe then they will become the powers that were. wouldn't that be fun?

———————

dear death,

oh no, you don't even think about it

———————

dear dentist,

kindly tell your patients to be patient & don't chew on their tongues. it could be regarded as rude & may harm your practice in the long run. run far & run free. later tonight the lights go on

---

dear depression,

you're all good & well as a term in geology. but the psychologigal affliction is asked to stay the hell away from my near & dear ones & everyone else for that matter

---

dear driver,

i fear this will have to be rather long. there are so many things you need to learn. like how sidewalks aren't for driving. like how sidewalks aren't for driving. like how sidewalks aren't for driving. like how sidewalks aren't for driving. like how sidewalks aren't for driving. like how sidewalks aren't for driving. like how sidewalks aren't for driving. like how sidewalks aren't for driving. like how sidewalks aren't for driving. like how sideWALKS aren't for driving. like how sidewalks aren't for driving. like how sidewalks aren't for driving. like how sidewalks aren't for driving. like how sidewalks aren't for driving. like how sidewalks aren't for driving. & another rather important thing. like how the brakes are as useful as the accelerator. like how the brakes are as useful as the accelerator. like how the brakes are as useful as the accelerator. like how the brakes are as useful as the accelerator. like how the brakes are as useful as the accelerator. like how the brakes are as useful as the accelerator. like how the brakes are as useful as the accelerator. like how the brakes are as useful as the accelerator. like how the brakes are as useful as the accelerator. like how the brakes are as useful as the accelerator. like how the brakes are as useful as the accelerator. like how the brakes are as useful as the accelerator. like how the brakes are as useful as the accelerator. like how the brakes are as useful as the accelerator. like how the brakes are as useful as the accelerator

---

dear god,

if you want my immoral soul you can have it. i don't believe in it

---

dear government,

how can it be that you never resigned?

---

dear haiku,

this is not one of you

dear head,

don't fail me now. i need you to serve poetry

---

dear immortality,

why not? though not my mortal coil please. you can have the scribbles

---

dear mail,

that thump on the hall floor still beats the electronic variety. & when the mailman is a madman from swansea you take on another social dimension

---

dear missionary,

your sexual position may be the most popular in the world, i'll give you that much

---

dear mothers,

once upon a time a pram was primarily used to transport your infants not for pushing pedestrians aside

_____

dear nazis,

die. now

_____

dear otitis,

would you please stay away? i've had quite enough of you

_____

dear pacu,

a nut is not necessarily a nut & if you want it vegetarian you need to make sure there are no limbs attached to it which would be fairly easy unless you're completely devoid of sense(s)

_____

dear pen or pencil,

you're great for sketches, in literary language, drafts. as the first vessel for a new piece of something or other. i am partial to the pen, a basic ballpoint for all purposes from scribbles to crossword puzzles because you don't have the easy possibility of erasing

---

dear piano,

you sound surprisingly good for being so out of tune. maybe that has something to do with who's playing you

---

dear poetry,

you took me by surprise 31 years ago & you haven't ceased to amaze me since

---

dear politician,

may i humbly suggest you stop evading relevant questions. stop lying. & maybe most importantly stop taking from the poor & giving to the rich. there are lots of other things as well. but these should be the easy ones to start with. right?

dear poverty,

you are history. you just don't know it yet. & neither do those who profit from you. or most anyone else. it's quite possible that only some who live in you sense the possibility or necessity of terminating you. but you should be aware that you're history

---

dear public service,

is it not time for you to return to living up to your name? it's been so long

---

dear red flag,

why is the young man you share balcony with looking so sad &/or tired?

---

dear reggae artist,

your backbeat is contagious & takes me from this pale northern land & for that i thank you kindly & ask that you keep doing what you're doing

---

dear shopping mall,

please relax. you will get your 30 silver coins

---

dear sleep,

i suggest you refrain from playing hide & seek

---

dear snowball,

don't go to hell. you'll be doomed. don't go anywhere near me. you'll be doomed

---

dear someone,

shall we do something somewhat strange sometime to some body or other?

---

dear summer,

come back. i love you madly. all is forgiven. though there was never anything to forgive. except maybe you leaving us for dead every year. i'm ready now. you may come tomorrow if you can't today

---

dear sun,

you do too many good things to mention here. so just a few. you bring life, both literally & figuratively speaking. you bring energy & smiles to the people who see too little of you. without you there would be no shade for those in need of that. without you there would be no charter travels. no need for sun block, nothing to dry up the city streets after the rain, no sunspots for m i a to write a song about. without you there would be nothing much at all. just so you know

---

dear synesthesia,

when a kid i thought nothing of you unless i expressed you. I didn't even know your name. years later i thought you slightly weird. nowadays you're just there making the way i sense the world a bit more interesting & probably richer than it might have been without you

---

dear techno nerd,

you know there is something called social context

---

dear thunder,

we love it when you do your collaboration with lightning at night. then your show gets really great

---

dear time,

you are a force of your own. a movement, artistic or other. there are many strange things said about you. most westerners love to complain they don't have enough of you to seem popular &/or important

---

dear water,

maybe i'm amazed as a song by the pixies is called that people drink you bathe in you cook in you desalinate & flavour you so you'll taste better water plants & lawns with you even start wars over you but when you come down to us in drops from clouds people run from you in something resembling terror & if they cant hide they unfold umbrellas designed solely to keep you off them dear well-digger

i do believe you need some warmer pants

---

dear westerners,

could we try to learn some basic humanity so we might stop being accidents

---

dear wheel,

what do you say me & anarchism meet tomorrow at 11.55 am & reinvent you

---

dear zebra,

if you were stripped of your stripes, what would you call yourself?

(hastings)

continuing the breakfast habits of contemporary europeans we get to the french abroad with one of them removing most of the bread from inside a bun before adding cheese & salami while another one cuts open a water melon with a tableknife

last days of april parched streets oblivious of shakespeare & company advising "be not inhospitable to strangers lest they be angels in disguise"

mark my words with a red & black marker pen & then forget them & if this is a guide you may shape it yourself & it most certainly isn't about politics this time

how about we draw a drinkable cup of coffee for that toothpaste thief sentenced to turn around to face a blood moon

iridium flash

foaming at the mouth of a laughing dog leaping down a flight of stairs at a kid on an electric skateboard or a burning math book

this is how you destroy that which destroys you

i hate maths though i like cooking my family & my pets & how to put words on a town so amorphous & a population so difficult to envision anywhere else?

this door is a jar of red table wine

not to mention those mansions down on millionaires row where those millionaires come & go not thinking of michelangelo whispering i have no god live with it

is it the day that's random?

or a car called khaled

probably not the same one who planted a large patch of garlic in the park & then spent the night as a bar owner in some small mexican town

at the bottom of the drink list "molotov cocktail for outside use"

so tell me how does being sentenced to 500 years in prison for a 500 page poem need any more context than that?

distill the life that's inside of me

serve in a nice glass

hold the ice & enjoy out of reach of the surprisingly bright spring sun

or these *hardcore bosnians on tour* having driven from tuzla to paris to watch their national football team beat france in the final european qualifier being slightly less expansive when we returned to the hotel at about 1.30 a.m

this plane forced to land in england by farting cows

learning fragments of another local language

& that public transport system forced karl & friedrich to move a handful of yards to the east

& the sweet madness in planning a high speed railway line from north east china to the continental u s

loop zero

this is how you argue safely

this is how your face gets cut into cubes

this is how you barbeque your self

your shelf returns seasons seasoned without authority

& of course mr. science works with making robots cooperate with humans in factories & of course the studies include violence

& time to tune that piano in the corner & steal that guitar for the book is handed out for free

& the road side littered with walking dead

& her constant paranoia

every weapon is a tool

& all the people who built that pyramid

& oi the punks are with us

& the first gang of the day marching from the square

& habitats painted red

& that tv squeezed into a corner between couch & chair & covered with pillows & blankets

& talk of agony & revolution

& all cops are bastards & once again they showed that

& all these people facing the same book

& going left of the roses & what's left of the roses

& kangaroos fighting in the street

& a mouth chewing trees

in the quiet area no one is allowed to breathe or even scribble in the old fashioned way

& my hand became a monster again

& he's quite sure he imagines

& if his memory serves him well he never saw the rather large banner saying something about loving someone in real (such as it is around here) life

be tray

meanwhile in istanbul a poet who camped for weeks in ghezi tells a reporter that lemon is good for those tear gas bombs

how about that green bulb near the periphery of your vision?

waiting in the shade to get in & start making paella

waiting in the shadows to turn someone into a paella

asking if this is election or erection day

the rule of vengeance

should you dream of anyone i know, give them my regards

the rule of law

the various laws of physics & the jungle throwing its legislators to the lions who look disdainfully at them & return them for you to enjoy irresponsibly

getting that brogue in order

in my rebellious youth i

wait i'm still heading into it

we are the soma mine explosion killing upward of 300 workers

you must fear your new shoes

we are formaldehyde

it speaks with forked tongues

it uses tongues as forks in the road rather than planting them in the spine of a not fictional dog

& we can only speculate how but the sun sent the clouds running

but oh the horror

hindu fascists win this election in india

& northern europe votes their fascists into the european parliament

while the south voted left & spain said we can

we are everywhere

this lady letting her twin daughters run some of their excessive energy off in the sunny square

& suddenly they get 15 afghan teenage sons

& suddenly they reap the blue lights & go to market

& suddenly they don't quite know what to do with the voices down in the street at 1.30 a.m on a warm thursday night

& suddenly they decide to cut the cat in half just be cause they can instead of opening another can of worms lest they find themselves by a quay fishing & finishing loading that ship with their catch of the day

light saving sanity

don't try to get out of your face

it seems your face wants to keep you

through another town with no discernible name on another open road tail lights snake off ahead in to another entertaining day into another mountain pass

passing the friday unaware bakunin had his 200th birthday as if he cared

yet 2 attentive anarchists celebrated him

we are oppositional defiant disorder

we are running down that hill

& what to do with that piece of string?

www.ingramcontent.com/pod-product-compliance
Lightning Source LLC
Chambersburg PA
CBHW022125040426
42450CB00006B/857